GUY TALK

Lizzie Cox

Illustrations by Damien Weighill

QED

CONTENTS

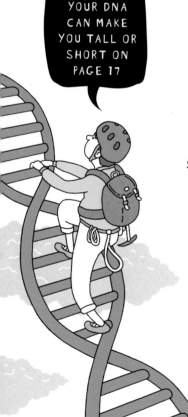

LEARN HOW YOUR DNA CAN MAKE YOU TALL OR SHORT ON PAGE 17

FIND OUT ABOUT
SKINCARE ON
PAGE 20

DISCOVER
THE SECRETS
OF YOUR
PENIS ON
PAGE 10

Quarto is the authority on a wide range of topics.
Quarto educates, entertains and enriches the lives of
our readers—enthusiasts and lovers of hands-on living.
www.quartoknows.com

Author: Lizzie Cox
Illustrator: Damien Weighill
Consultant: John Rees
Editor: Alice Bowden
Designer: Tracy Killick
QED Editor: Carly Madden
QED Designer: Victoria Kimonidou

Copyright © QED Publishing 2017

First published in the UK in 2017 by
QED Publishing
Part of The Quarto Group
The Old Brewery, 6 Blundell Street,
London, N7 9BH

A catalogue record for this book is available from
the British Library.

ISBN 978 1 78493 829 1

Printed in China

MIX
Paper from
responsible sources
FSC® C101537
FSC
www.fsc.org

THE P-WORD: PUBERTY

You've probably heard people talking about 'going through puberty', but what on earth does that 'P' word mean? **PUBERTY** is the name for all the changes your body goes through as you grow from a boy into a man. **DRUMROLL, PLEASE.**

You've been growing ever since you were born (obviously, otherwise you'd still be rolling around on the floor in a nappy), but it's when you reach puberty that you'll notice the biggest changes happening to your body. Changes that affect you physically *and* emotionally.

Dropping the ball!

The term 'balls dropping' is slang for a boy starting puberty and beginning to produce sperm. However, your testicles don't **ACTUALLY** drop! They descended into your scrotum ages ago – before you were five years old!

Changes like getting taller, growing hair in places there **DEFINITELY** wasn't hair before, and feeling feelings that are totally new to you.

All aboard!

All sounds like quite a lot to deal with, doesn't it? Well **HAVE NO FEAR** – by the end of this book you'll be clued up about what's going to happen, and fully prepared for the puberty train.

```
88074012   ★ ★ ★ ★ ★ ★
           ONE-WAY TICKET
           PUBERTY TRAIN
           ★ ★ ★ ★ ★ ★   88074012
```

The beginning

Most boys begin puberty anywhere between the ages of 9 and 15, but some will start seeing changes earlier, and some later – puberty is different for everyone.

The rate at which all these changes happen also differs from person to person. Some boys might go through puberty in a year or less, while others take a few years to finish fully developing.

When does it start?

The important thing to remember is that there's no set or 'normal' time for puberty to begin. So you can put that calendar away – circling a date and writing '**PUBERTY STARTS**' won't work here. Sorry!

YIPPEE!

When it comes to puberty there is no right or wrong: it happens when it happens, and it takes as long as it takes. What we're trying to say is **DON'T PANIC** or worry about developing before or after your friends – it all evens out in the end.

BUT... <u>WHAT</u> MAKES PUBERTY HAPPEN?

Are you ready for **THE SCIENCE BIT**? *dramatic music*. It's all about hormones — chemicals in your body that travel around in the blood telling your cells and organs to do certain things. Think of them as little chemical messengers that kickstart puberty, then carry on telling your body how to develop and change as you become an adult.

HORMONE NINJAS!

STAGE 1 It all starts when one of those hormones we talked about travels to a pea-sized place at the base of your brain, called the pituitary gland. This hormone arrives and tells the gland to release new, different hormones, including one called testosterone from your testicles (sometimes called '**BALLS**', because they're... well, sort of ball shaped). Your testicles then start producing sperm, the male cell that creates a baby when it meets a female egg. You'll also start to get taller, often shooting up suddenly, in what is known as a 'growth spurt'.

JUST HOW LONG HAVE I BEEN ASLEEP?

STAGE 2 As you continue to get taller and heavier, your testicles will also begin growing larger, and fine hair will start to grow at the base of your penis. This is known as pubic hair.

GREAT BALLS OF FIRE!

STAGE 3 Your penis will begin to get longer. Boys' voices often start to get deeper at this stage too, which is sometimes known as your voice 'breaking'. **DON'T WORRY**, it's not actually broken! It might go a bit wobbly and squeaky every now and then, but this is totally normal — it'll settle down as you continue to develop.

STAGE 4 Pubic hair carries on growing and your penis will get thicker as well as longer. Skin starts to become oilier, which can cause spots (see pp. **20–23**). Hair will also start growing under your arms and on your upper lip and chin. Yep, you're entering **MOUSTACHE TERRITORY** now!

Did you know?

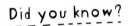

Many boys notice swelling or tenderness around one or both nipples when they hit puberty. But don't panic — you're not turning into a woman — it's just your hormones racing about and is only temporary, usually lasting just a few months.

STAGE 5 As puberty comes to an end, you'll reach your full adult height, and your shoulders will get wider. Facial hair will grow regularly, and you might decide to start shaving (see pp. **18–19**). Physically, you are now a **MAN**.

THE BRAIN GAME

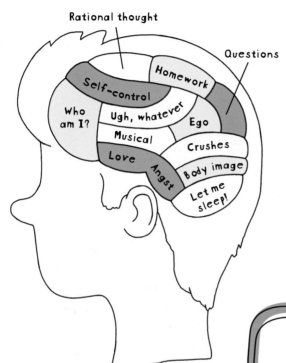

Rational thought

Questions

Self-control

Homework

Who am I?

Ugh, whatever

Ego

Musical

Crushes

Love

Angst

Body image

Let me sleep!

It's not just your outside that changes when you hit puberty – your insides are changing too, including your brain.

The biggest development happens in the front area of your brain, called the **FRONTAL LOBE**. The frontal lobe is a bit of a bossy boots and basically tells the rest of your brain what to do. It isn't fully developed until you've finished puberty.

This means that as you start the physical changes – getting taller, growing pubic hair, and so on – you'll also become more **GROWN-UP** emotionally as your brain develops. It is being reshaped to become more efficient, like someone pruning a tree to make it grow better. But while the pruning is happening, you might feel like your emotions keep getting the better of you.

Manage your moods

TAKE A BREAK. Feel upset or angry? Find a quiet spot, take some deep breaths, and concentrate on something that makes you happy.

SNOOZE. When going through puberty you need a lot of sleep so you don't get grouchy. Try and get at least 8 hours sleep a night.

APOLOGISE. Everyone says things they don't mean sometimes, it's life – but an apology can make everything feel better.

What's going on in my <u>brain</u>?

Different areas of your brain start to connect more, and at the same time new brain connections are being made.

Brain pathways that you use a lot (like working out how to reach level two of your favourite computer game) start speeding up.

Old brain pathways that you hardly ever use (like playing with Lego) close down.

Your emotions work faster than the bit of the brain that controls them, so they can feel a bit out of control sometimes.

Getting emotional

What do you get when you take all of those new <u>hormones</u> having a party in your bloodstream, and combine them with your growing brain? A load of brand new emotions and feelings, that's what.

Puberty can be overwhelming, and you might find yourself having stronger and more extreme emotions. These are sometimes called 'MOOD SWINGS', because you may feel fine one minute, and then really sad or angry the next.

The important thing to keep in mind is that this is N.O.R.M.A.L. You're in between being a boy and a man, and that's a lot to deal with. It's not surprising you might sometimes feel moody, or even angry.

THE OTHER P-WORD: PENISES

Ready, set, **PENISES**. Yup, it's time to talk all things 'down there', so put down that hot-dog you're having for lunch and listen up. Being a boy, you've probably already got a whole lot of questions about penises. And with puberty heading your way, you need to prepare for some changes. So here's everything you need to know about your penis.

HEY, GUYS, WHAT'S SO FUNNY?

Did you know?

FUN FACT ALERT: your penis is actually shaped like a boomerang! Only half of its length is actually visible outside of your body. Just like a tree, the penis also has a sort of root you can't see, inside your pelvis and attached to your pubic bone.

Penises have two basic functions

1. To get rid of wee (urine).
2. To allow you to reproduce (that means to have children), in the future. It does this by passing sperm from the testicles into a woman's uterus during sex.

Penises grow at different rates

As your body starts going through puberty, your penis will grow both longer and wider over time. **HOWEVER**, everyone develops at a different pace. Your penis may reach full size as early as age 13, or as late as age 21.

So basically, don't stress if you feel like your mates are growing up quicker than you – puberty is a stubborn old thing, and won't hurry up, even if you want it to.

There is no 'normal' size or shape

You know what the best part about being human is? We come in **ALL KINDS** of shapes, sizes and colours. How boring (and confusing) would it be if we all looked identical? The same goes for penises – no two are the same. The size of your penis depends on your **DNA**, just like the size of your feet or the colour of your hair.

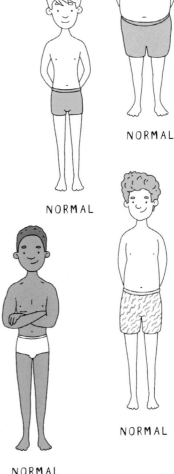

NORMAL

NORMAL

NORMAL

NORMAL

Small talk

A lot of boys worry that their penis is too small, but size really isn't something that you should stress out about! As we've already discussed, everyone grows at different rates – and most penises are around the same size when they are erect (hard), even if they look smaller when flaccid (soft).

Foreskin vs. circumcision

All boys are born with a foreskin – a little fold of skin that goes around the head of the penis, sort of like a little fleshy scarf.

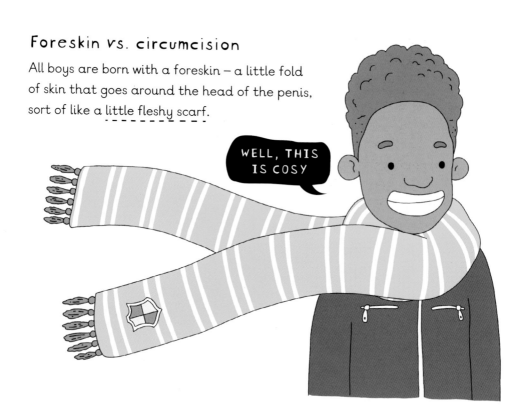

WELL, THIS IS COSY

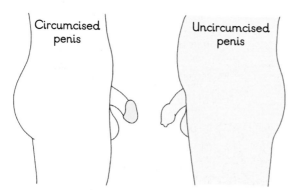

Circumcised penis

Uncircumcised penis

CIRCUMCISION is when parents choose to have a baby's foreskin surgically removed, leaving the head of the penis exposed. Reasons parents might decide to do this include religious beliefs, or because it's easier to keep clean.

Some boys also have to be circumcised for medical reasons. For example, if they are born with a condition that means the foreskin can't be pulled back, or is too tight around the head of the penis.

This doesn't mean that a penis with a foreskin is dirty! In fact, the whole point of it being there is to **PROTECT** your penis. Keeping it clean is easy; just pull the fold of skin gently down when you wash. Both circumcised and uncircumcised penises still work the same way – whether you have a foreskin or not doesn't change that.

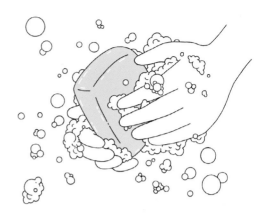

I have a question!

 My penis seems to get smaller when it's cold. Is this normal?

Yep, totally normal. All penises shrink by up to 50 per cent in cold water or weather! Your body preserves heat in cold temperatures by keeping the blood flowing around your important internal organs, and reducing blood flow to the bits that aren't actually keeping you alive, like your fingers, toes and penis.

 I've noticed some white bumps on the skin at the head of my penis.

DON'T PICK or try to **SQUEEZE** them – you'll damage the sensitive skin of your penis. These white or yellow bumps are called papules, and lots of boys and men get them. They're usually nothing to worry about but if they hurt, or are red and itchy, get checked out by your doctor.

 I keep getting white stuff under my foreskin. What is it?

Don't panic – this white stuff is called smegma, and it's also perfectly normal – it's your body's way of keeping your foreskin naturally lubricated. Make sure you (gently!) clean behind your foreskin every day to keep the head of your penis squeaky clean, and to stop the smegma from starting to smell or itch.

IT'S A HARD LIFE

Erections happen when blood fills the penis, making it hard (and easier to insert into the woman's vagina). Yup, your erection is basically a sausage-shaped sack of blood. <u>Lovely</u>.

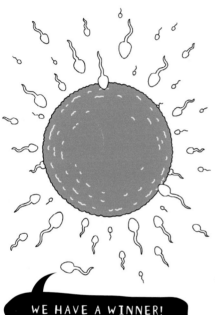

WE HAVE A WINNER!

Erections also make it possible for your body to ejaculate. What's ejaculation? Good question. Ejaculation is when **SEMEN**, a white liquid containing sperm, shoots out the end of your penis. When a man and woman have sex, this semen then enters the woman's uterus. If a sperm meets an egg released from the woman's ovary, then the two together can make a baby.

YEE-HA!

Surprise erections

Erections are your body's way of preparing for sex, and so mostly happen when you're aroused. However...**HERE COMES PUBERTY** trying to screw up your life again...sometimes you can get surprise erections.

Oh yes: almost all boys going through puberty will experience erections at totally random times, when nothing even a little bit sexy is happening. On the school bus, in class, walking down the street – there's no telling when one might pop up.

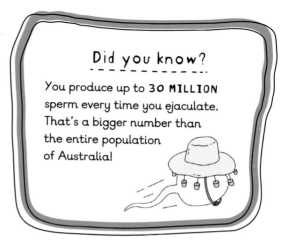

Did you know?

You produce up to **30 MILLION** sperm every time you ejaculate. That's a bigger number than the entire population of Australia!

There's not a lot you can do about this other than wait it out, and perhaps carry around a big folder for 'cover up' emergencies. One thing you should <u>never</u> do, though, is try and force an erection down – this can cause penile fractures (**AAGH!**).

Wet dreams

Ah, another wonderful penis-related part of puberty: having a <u>sexy dream</u> and waking up to find that you've ejaculated during the night and there's now semen all over the sheets.

First up: **DON'T BE EMBARRASSED** – this happens to pretty much **ALL** boys at some stage during puberty. It's a natural part of growing up, and there's nothing to be ashamed of. Might be worth asking mum, dad or big bro how to use the washing machine, though!

GROWING PAINS

When puberty really gets going it can feel like your body is changing every day – and that can feel a bit strange, like you don't even know yourself from one day to the next! It's also easy to start **COMPARING YOURSELF** to other boys your age, wondering why you're not as tall as Paul, or as big as Ben.

I WISH I WASN'T THIS TALL! I WANT TO BE LIKE EVERYONE ELSE

WHAT A GIANT – HE MAKES ME FEEL TINY!

EVERYONE worries about their body at some stage, asking themselves if they're tall enough, or muscular enough, or hairy enough – the important thing to remember is that everyone is different and that's fine. Make the most of who you are, and be **HAPPY**.

Watch out, clumsy

As your arms and legs grow longer – sometimes quite suddenly – they can feel slightly alien. You might be a bit clumsy for a while, tripping up or knocking things. Your body and brain need time to adjust to these new changes. Once your muscles, weight and shoulders naturally bulk up, they'll help even things out.

Muscle men

Don't stress yourself out thinking that you need a six-pack and big ol' biceps. It's not actually natural for teenage boys to have huge muscles, and body-building or extreme weight-lifting is dangerous for your growing body. Yes, keep fit by playing sports and being active, but don't worry about piling on the muscles – these will develop naturally as puberty moves along.

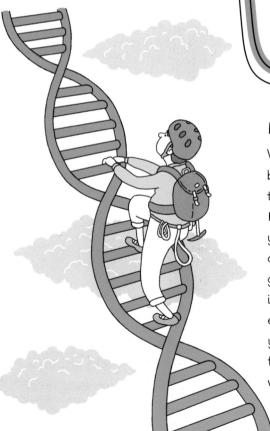

How tall?

We've already established that all boys grow at different rates, but how tall you'll end up depends on your **DNA**. This is the special genetic code you inherited from both your parents, a code which tells your body how to grow and look. You can get a general idea of how tall or short you might end up by looking at the height of your mum and dad. But this isn't a fixed indicator, so you'll just have to wait and find out. Sorry!

17

HAIR WE GO

When puberty hits, so does hair growth. In fact, it can seem like it's popping up and getting thicker **EVERYWHERE** – on your face, underarms, legs, chest and down <u>there</u>.

Age 9

Age 12

Age 15

The hair around your penis and testicles is known as 'pubic' hair because it sits on the pubic bone... clever. It's usually more curly and wiry than the hair on your head.

Shaving: what, when and how?

As you continue down the puberty path to becoming a man, you'll start to grow hair on your face. This usually starts with your upper lip, then your chin and jaw. Some boys will find that the hair is thick, dark and grows quite quickly, while others have something that looks more like 'fuzz' – much finer, lighter hair – or barely any hair at all.

IT WASN'T LIKE THIS WHEN I WENT TO BED LAST NIGHT!

☰ Shaving tips ☰

1. **NEVER** share your razor with someone else, and **ALWAYS** use foam or gel when shaving to avoid an itchy rash or cutting yourself.

2. Shave in a **DOWNWARDS** direction, using long and even strokes – and don't press too hard!

3. Shave your cheeks and chin first, then your top lip. Curling your lip under your teeth to pull your skin tighter helps when tackling this bit.

4. Change your razor **REGULARLY** to avoid it getting all germy and gross.

MUCHO MOUSTACHE

Guess what, though? It's all **NORMAL**. Don't ever worry that you're not developing properly because you haven't got a big ol' moustache – not having loads of facial hair doesn't make you any less of a man.

REMEMBER
- - - - - - -
Hair styling products aren't just for girls. Loads of guys use wax, gel or mousse to style their locks as well as hair dye and hair dryers. After all, why should girls have all the fun?

Chest hair or all bare?

While many men leave their chest hair as it is, some men decide to remove it. Neither option is better than the other. It's a personal choice! But just so you know, body hair is actually really important. It keeps you warm, protects your skin from germs or bacteria, and creates a barrier to reduce friction between you and your clothes.

SPOTS & SKIN

All those puberty hormones make your skin produce more oil, which clogs up your **PORES** (tiny little holes in your skin – look reeeeally closely and you'll see them). This can cause spots on your face, neck, shoulders and back. In more extreme cases, this can also lead to acne.

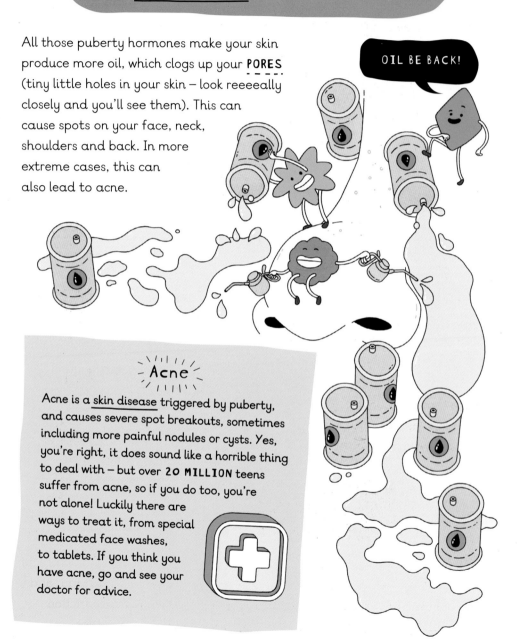

OIL BE BACK!

Acne

Acne is a <u>skin disease</u> triggered by puberty, and causes severe spot breakouts, sometimes including more painful nodules or cysts. Yes, you're right, it does sound like a horrible thing to deal with – but over **20 MILLION** teens suffer from acne, so if you do too, you're not alone! Luckily there are ways to treat it, from special medicated face washes, to tablets. If you think you have acne, go and see your doctor for advice.

Spot the difference

Unlike humans, not all spots are created equal; there are actually different types. Here's how to **SPOT** (**HA HA!**) each kind, and how to deal with it.

Whiteheads

These are small spots with whitish yellow 'heads' filled with pus, **YUCK**. They can be (gently) squeezed, but wash your hands first, or squeeze between a piece of clean tissue. If you have germs on your fingers, you'll create **MORE** spots.

Blackheads

See any tiny black or brown pin pricks? These are blackheads. They're blocked pores that are 'open'. The black colour is created when the <u>bacteria</u> inside reacts with the air around you. You can damage your skin if you try to squeeze these. The best way to get rid of them is to use a gentle face wash every morning and evening.

> HEY BUDDY, YOU'RE ABOUT TO GET CREAMED!

Papules

These suckers are red, painful spots under the skin, created when trapped oil and bacteria have caused inflammation. They should definitely <u>**NOT**</u> be squeezed – just keep them clean and apply some spot cream.

Give your skin some TLC

Because your skin is extra prone to spots when you hit puberty, you **NEED NEED NEED** to make sure you're cleaning it properly, and giving it some **TLC** (that's tender loving care, duh).

1. Wash your face with a **GENTLE CLEANSER** in the morning <u>AND</u> at night, making sure not to scrub too hard (this can hurt your skin and make it sore).

2. Moisturise, moisturise, **MOISTURIIIISE**. You might think that all that skin oil means you don't need more moisture, but you do! If your skin gets too dry, it can produce even **MORE** oil, which means more spots.

3. You can then apply some **MEDICATED CREAM** from the chemist to any spots. Make sure it's not too strong; you don't want to irritate your skin. You can always ask for advice in the chemist to find which product is best for you.

Wash your towels and pillowcases every two weeks, to get rid of **GERMS**.

Try not to touch your face with dirty fingers.

It might sound odd, but if you wear glasses, wash them with water and soap regularly, to stop spot-making grease building up.

SQUEAKY CLEAN...

...ALL OVER!

Exfoliate!

It's not just your face that needs **TLC**! Look after the skin on your body by using a gentle exfoliator when you shower. This is a body wash with little scrubbing particles in it that remove dead skin cells and dirt, helping to reduce spots that can pop up on your back and shoulders during puberty.

Did you know?

It isn't 'girly' to look after your skin. Loads of boys and men are into skin care, which is why there are so many great skin products on the market, **ESPECIALLY** for guys!

23

FACE IT: EYES & TEETH

As you grow you need to take care of all your body's bits and bobs, from the top of your head to the tips of your toes. This includes your eyes and teeth. They're pretty important, what with being responsible for your eyesight, keeping your breath fresh and giving you a great smile!

Glasses

Lots of people need glasses to help them see. If you find yourself squinting, or things look a little blurry, talk to an adult about going for an **EYE TEST**.

An optician will check out your eyesight using some <u>fun tests</u> involving lights, mirrors and lenses (don't worry, none are painful!). They can then tell you if you need glasses.

I AM SO ROCKING THE CLARK KENT LOOK

REMEMBER

You might feel a bit strange or embarrassed wearing glasses at first, but you shouldn't be. Glasses are cool – just ask Harry Potter! WINGARDIUM LEVIOSA.

Contact lenses

Some people choose to wear contacts instead. These are little curved lenses that you place on your eyeball and are pretty much **INVISIBLE**. They must be cleaned <u>very carefully</u> to avoid infection. If you want to try contacts, speak to your optician.

Did you know?

You are born with two sets of teeth inside your mouth! The adult teeth that push out your baby teeth as you grow are present from birth, hidden up inside your gums.

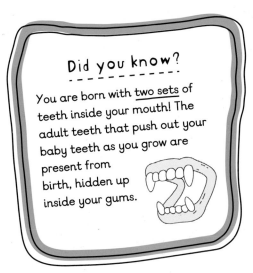

Braces

If your teeth are a bit wonky or overcrowded, you might need braces. A special dentist called an **ORTHODONTIST** fits these, and you can have them for a few months or a few years, depending on how much your teeth need to move.

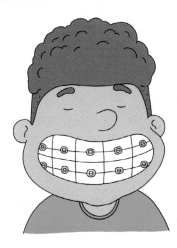

Keeping your teeth squeaky <u>clean</u>

BRUSH TWICE A DAY: every morning and again before bed.

GENTLY BRUSH YOUR GUMS with a circular motion when cleaning your teeth to keep gums strong. Scrub your tongue too to get rid of germs that make breath smell.

FLOSS. Remove all those bits of food and bacteria stuck between your teeth.

VISIT YOUR DENTIST twice a year. Yes, it's scary, but you have to go!

AVOID FIZZY DRINKS, your teeth hate the sugar. Don't brush your teeth just after drinking fizzy pop or juice: this can wear away their protective coating.

There are different types of braces: some are clear and plastic, some are like metal bars and some are brackets glued to the front of each tooth, with a wire running in between. You may feel self-conscious to begin with, but it'll all be worth it when you have lovely straight teeth!

B. O. &
PERSONAL HYGIENE

Sweat is a part of life. In fact, if we didn't sweat we'd be in real trouble, as perspiring (that's just a fancy word for 'sweating') is needed to cool our bodies down and stop them from overheating.

B.O.

Ready to learn about body odour? The first thing you need to know is that you have two types of **SWEAT GLANDS**. The first type work from the moment you're born, but the second type only start functioning during puberty – it sort of wakes them up, the lazy little things.

The second type of gland releases natural oils, which react with bacteria on your skin and cause body odour, also known as B.O. **POOOO-EY.**

YOU STINK!

Now that you have more sweat glands working (around three million in total!) you'll also notice that you start to sweat more, especially under your arms. **B.O. CAN SMELL REALLY BAD,** so it's important that you keep clean and fresh.

Hygiene

Keep B.O. away by washing regularly. You should take a **SHOWER** at least every other day, and especially after you play sport or just get very sweaty.

A quick rinse won't get rid of all that bacteria on your skin! Lather up some soap or shower gel and wash your body all over. You can also start using a gentle anti-perspirant deodorant under your arms to stop the sweat smell.

I have a question!

 Should I wash my penis and testicles with soap too?

Yes, it can get pretty sweaty down there. When you shower, gently wash your testicles and pull back your foreskin (if you have one) as you wash your penis – just don't **SCRUB!** These parts are delicate and you don't want to damage them!

 How can I make sure I don't smell?

Deodorant is your biggest friend, as well as washing your body and hair properly. Dirty clothes can also pong, as they absorb germs and sweat. Change your underwear every day, and drop clothes in the laundry basket after you've worn them a couple of times.

ALL THINGS FEET

Feet are one of the first parts of your body to feel the effects of puberty, and can grow two or three sizes in a short space of time – so maybe hold off buying those expensive trainers just yet!

Your feet reach full size about a year before you get to full adult height and weight. So when your feet stop growing, you know you're nearly there.

What's that smell?

Just like the rest of your body, your feet have lots of sweat glands. And just like the rest of your body, you need to wash them regularly to stop them getting **WHIFFY**.

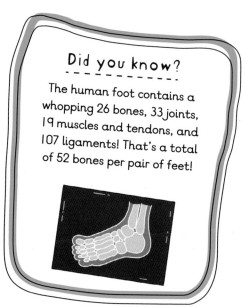

Did you know?

The human foot contains a whopping 26 bones, 33 joints, 19 muscles and tendons, and 107 ligaments! That's a total of 52 bones per pair of feet!

Beat the stink by:

1. Washing your feet every day, **AND** making sure you dry them properly before putting socks or shoes on.

2. Wearing a nice, clean pair of socks every day.

3. Making sure you let your feet breathe. Don't keep them wrapped up in shoes and socks all day, let them get some air for at least a couple of hours when you get home, and sleep barefoot.

4. Using scented insoles and foot powders (you can get these from your local chemist or supermarket).

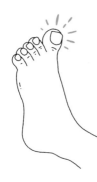

Ingrowing toenails

Ouch, ow and **AAGH**. Ingrown toenails happen when the corner or side of a toenail grows into the soft skin around it. It can be red, swollen and quite painful. It's important to treat these so that they don't get infected – if you think you might have a pesky ingrown nail, go and see your doctor.

Verrucas

Verrucas are actually just ordinary **WARTS**, forced to grow inwards because they're on the soles of your feet. They can be a bit painful, and will need to be treated with at-home medicine or by a doctor. They're also **VERY CONTAGIOUS**, and most commonly spread at swimming pools. If you have a verruca, wear a special rubber swimming sock, for the sake of us all.

YUCK!

Athlete's foot

Athlete's foot is a **FUNGAL INFECTION** that makes your feet all flaky and a bit gross! Fungus likes dark, damp and warm conditions – so make sure you change your sweaty socks as soon as you can. If you do get athlete's foot, it can be treated with an anti-fungal medicine.

29

GIRLS & PUBERTY

So what happens to girls when they hit puberty? Well, girls usually start developing earlier than boys do – between the ages of 8 and 14, which means that they have a head start and will often be taller (and more mature!) than boys in their class.

NO NEED TO TELL ME THAT BOYS ARE LESS MATURE!

Hormones – what's the difference?

Remember those bossy hormones telling your testes to start making testosterone? Well, for girls, they tell the ovaries to start making a new hormone called oestrogen. **OVARIES** are little sacs that hold eggs, and it is these eggs that may one day become a baby, when they are fertilized by a male's sperm.

The five stages of female puberty

STAGE 1 Once the ovaries start to produce oestrogen, the more noticeable physical changes begin and the body starts changing into a woman.

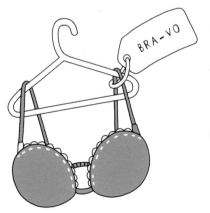

BRA-VO

STAGE 2 Girls get taller, begin to develop the first signs of breasts, and start growing underarm and pubic hair above and around the vulva (the entrance to the vagina).

STAGE 3 As girls continue to develop breasts and get taller, their hips will also get wider – this is to prepare their bodies for having a baby when they are grown up.

STAGE 4 Girls become fertile next. 'Fertile' is another way of saying 'able to have a baby', and means their ovaries will start releasing eggs, causing periods to start.

STAGE 5 Puberty ends when girls reach full adult height, their breasts have finished developing and their periods have started to follow a regular monthly pattern. Physically, they are now women. **PHEW!**

> **FINALLY, I AM COMING OUT OF MY SHELL**

Periods: the lowdown

Also called 'menstruation', a period is when blood from the uterus leaves the body through the vagina (*see p.39* for a diagram of girls' 'bits'). This usually happens between the ages of 10 and 14.

Each month an egg is released by one of the ovaries. It then travels down the **FALLOPIAN TUBE** to the uterus, which has been busy building a thin lining of blood and tissue along its walls in preparation for the egg's arrival.

If the egg isn't fertilized by a sperm before it enters the uterus, then the girl's body realises it's not pregnant and the lining breaks down, leaving her body as a period. That's what the blood is!

LOVE & RELATIONSHIPS

As puberty transforms you from boy to man, it's normal for you to start having new and strong feelings of <u>attraction</u> towards others. **OOH LA LA.**

These feelings can make you want to be close to someone you're attracted to. You might feel all warm and tingly (**EEEEE!**) when you think about that person being your girlfriend or boyfriend, or get all tongue-tied when you see them (thanks for that, brain!).

I REEAALLLLY LIKE HER!

Sometimes liking someone in this way is called '**HAVING A CRUSH**' on them. Developing your first real crush is an exciting – and **SCARY** – time. You're dealing with unfamiliar emotions and there's a whole load of questions buzzing around your brain.

Do they like me too? Can people **TELL** that I like them? What should I do about these feelings?

What to do with a crush

There are no set rules to follow – it's all about what you feel comfortable with. Talk to your friends about it if you like. These feelings are normal and natural, and you don't have to hide them. If you want to tell the person you like that you fancy them, that's fine. If you don't, that's fine too. You're the boss!

The science bit: hormones and L.O.V.E.

It's not just your body that changes during puberty, your brain has to do the same in order to keep up with your maturing body. This is why the hormones that change your body also change your emotions.

LOVE IS IN THE AIR!

As you go through puberty, you'll start to develop <u>romantic</u> and, later, sexual feelings towards other people. Just like everything else, this happens at different times for everyone.

33

What is a relationship?

Having a girlfriend or boyfriend – a.k.a. 'being in a relationship' – is a lot like friendship. You shouldn't feel pressured into doing anything you don't want to do, and you should feel <u>happy and safe</u>, not scared or uncomfortable.

Crushes: the good, the bad and the AAGH!

Having a crush can feel great... but bad, too. If someone doesn't like you back, or breaks up with you, it feels **RUBBISH.**

Crushes can also feel like an obsession – you **CAN'T. STOP. THINKING. ABOUT. THIS. PERSON,** and want to be near them **ALL. OF. THE. TIME.** These intense feelings might even seem as though they're taking over your life. **AAGH!**

Did you know?

It's also fine to **NOT** like anyone in this way. Don't fancy anyone? No problem. There's no law that says you have to want a boyfriend or girlfriend. Trust us, we checked.

I AM BROKEN – I WILL NEVER BE HAPPY AGAIN

Try to remember that you won't feel this way forever. You'll have lots of crushes in your lifetime, even if it seems as though this person is the only one for you right now.

I have a question!

I have feelings for another boy, not a girl – is this wrong?

Of course not! How could such positive feelings ever be wrong? Being attracted to people the same sex as you is known as being gay and it's nothing to be ashamed of. Lots of people have same-sex crushes during puberty, and while some boys only ever fancy boys, others discover they like both boys **AND** girls.

How do I make my crush like me?

You can't **MAKE** anyone like you. Be nice, friendly, and talk to them about your shared interests. Just be yourself! And remember: if they don't like you back, it might feel like the end of the world, but it's not. You **WILL** move on.

My friends are annoyed because I spend a lot of time with my girlfriend. What should I do?

Life is all about balance. It's great that you like this girl and want to spend time with her, but don't forget your friends! Friendship is for life, so make time for them too.

S.E.X. & HOW BABIES ARE MADE

When a man and a woman are attracted to each other, they might decide to have sexual intercourse, or 'sex' for short. When this happens, a man's erect penis is inserted into a woman's vagina. It's much more than that, though – it's about giving one another pleasure and enjoyment.

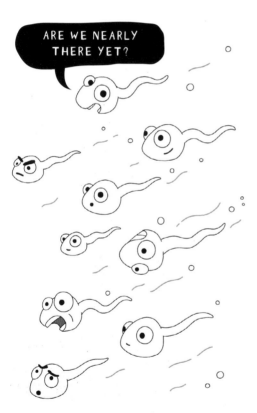

ARE WE NEARLY THERE YET?

I'M ALWAYS LATE FOR THE PARTY!

Sperm meets egg

During sex a man will ejaculate. This means that sperm comes out of his penis and is passed into the woman's vagina. The sperm swim through the cervix and into the woman's uterus where they head towards the fallopian tubes. The first sperm to meet an egg **WINS THE RACE**, burrowing inside. The egg is now 'fertilized' and begins to tumble down the fallopian tube to make its way to the uterus where it will embed itself into the wall of the womb, eventually becoming a baby.

Once a girl starts her **PERIODS**, it means she's able to get pregnant. It's illegal to have sex before you're 16 years old, because it's a step you should only take when you're fully matured, and emotionally as well as physically ready.

36

Contraception

Men and women have sex for fun (yep, really), not just to make babies. Using a contraception (also known as **'BIRTH CONTROL'**) prevents a man's sperm from fertilizing a woman's egg, so that she doesn't become pregnant.

CONDOMS are made from latex and roll onto a man's erect penis. The space at the end catches sperm and stops it passing into the vagina. You can buy these, but you can also get them for free from places such as schools, chemists and health clinics.

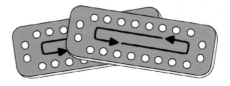

THE PILL is a hormone-based tablet that stops a woman's egg from attaching to the lining of her uterus. It must be taken by the woman every day to work effectively.

Orgasms

Intense feelings of pleasure during sex is called an orgasm. This happens for both men and women, and for men is accompanied by ejaculation. It's important that both men and women enjoy sex, and think about each other's needs!

WE'LL PLAN **THIS** TOGETHER

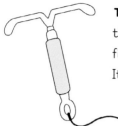

THE COIL: This is a plastic or metal device that looks a bit like the letter 'T', and sits inside a woman's uterus. It has to be fitted by a doctor, but can be left in place for up to 10 years! It stops eggs from attaching to the lining of the uterus.

THE IMPLANT: Some women choose to have the implant instead. This is about the size and shape of a hairgrip, and is placed just under the skin of the arm with a needle. It releases the same hormones used by the pill.

Implant

Boy parts: which bit is which?

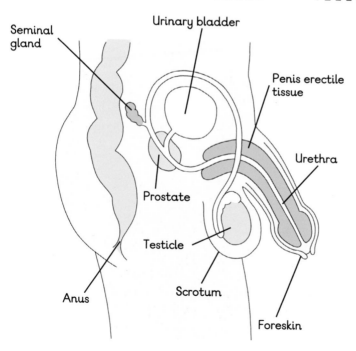

Seminal gland

Urinary bladder

Penis erectile tissue

Urethra

Prostate

Testicle

Scrotum

Anus

Foreskin

The parts shown here make up the male reproductive system. They work together to deliver sperm out of the body and into the vagina, where it can fertilize an egg to make a baby. The prostate gland acts as a sort of valve, which stops urine leaking out during ejaculation.

Girl parts: which bit is which?

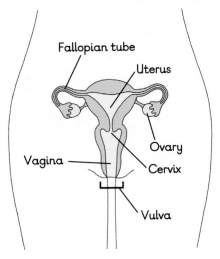

- Fallopian tube
- Uterus
- Ovary
- Cervix
- Vagina
- Vulva

The female reproductive system works to make it possible for the sperm to fertilize a woman's egg. It then prepares the body for the development of the foetus into a baby during pregnancy.

I have a question!

 Is it possible for a girl to get pregnant the first time she has sex?

YES, YES, YES! Girls can become pregnant as soon as their ovaries start releasing eggs. This means that even if they haven't started their periods, they could still get pregnant, as the egg is released before the bleeding starts for the first time.

 I want to have sex, but my girlfriend doesn't. What should we do?

NOBODY should have sex with another person until they are ready. It's a **HUGE** step and it shouldn't be rushed into. **NEVER** pressure anyone into going further than they want to. You should always respect your partner's decision.

 Someone has been touching me in ways I don't like. Is this OK?

NO. Nobody should **EVER** touch you without your consent. That means that if you haven't agreed to it, or don't want it to happen, they are **NOT** allowed to do it. Tell your parents or an adult you trust right away.

HEALTHY EATING & FITNESS

Your body is the most precious thing you have, and *SPOILER ALERT*: you only get one, so it's important to look after it. Stay healthy as you grow and develop by eating a nutritious and balanced diet.

REMEMBER

You should be eating three healthy meals a day: breakfast, lunch and dinner. Skipping meals isn't a good idea – your body works hard, and it needs fuel to keep it going, just like a car.

WHAT'S A BALANCED DIET?

Oh, we're so glad you asked. A balanced diet means eating a variety of foods containing the various <u>vitamins</u> and <u>nutrients</u> your body needs.

Eat a lot of...

FRUIT AND VEGETABLES: Packed with <u>goodness</u>, you should eat at least five portions a day.

CARBOHYDRATES: Potatoes, pasta, rice, beans and brown bread keep your <u>energy levels</u> up.

DAIRY: Milk, cheese and yoghurt contain calcium, essential for keeping growing bones <u>strong</u>.

PROTEIN: Chicken, fish, soy, tofu, nuts and eggs are all packed with protein and are needed to maintain and <u>build muscles</u> you use every day.

BITE ME, DUDE!

40

Eat a little of...

SUGARY FOODS: Sweets, chocolate and fizzy drinks **SHOULDN'T** be part of your everyday diet!

SALTY SNACKS: Junk food and crisps have **LOADS** of salt, so save them for treats only. Too much salt can raise your blood pressure, which is bad for your heart, liver and kidneys.

Eating disorders

An eating disorder is when someone develops an unhealthy and dangerous relationship with food. This may mean that they stop eating almost completely – a condition called ANOREXIA. Or they may make themselves sick, which is a condition known as BULIMIA.

Another eating disorder is BODY DYSMORPHIA. No matter how much weight a person loses, they still see themselves as 'fat'. Eating disorders lead to serious health problems and even death. If you have issues with food, PLEASE talk to someone who can help you.

Exercise

Keeping active is just as important as good food when it comes to staying healthy. Walking, running and playing sports are all great ways to exercise. You should do something that gets your heart pumping for at least 30 minutes a day. No, that doesn't include watching scary films.

HE SHOOTS, HE SCORES!

BODY IMAGE

Well, it's all about how you see yourself, and how you feel about yourself. Having a **HEALTHY, POSITIVE BODY IMAGE** means accepting who you are and feeling comfortable in your own skin. Sounds great, right?

All shapes and sizes

When puberty shows up and starts doing its thing, everyone's bodies change in different ways. Some are tall, some are short, some are big, some are small – but all are human, and no one body type is better than another.

Having a positive body image is nothing to do with shape or size, and everything to do with how **YOU** feel about yourself. There is no 'perfect' or 'ideal' way a boy or man should look.

Get that positive body image feeling

LOVE YOURSELF. You are the only you there is, and that's a good thing. Love the skin you're in and remember: life is about being happy and having fun, not about looking a certain way.

ROCKIN' IT!

REMEMBER

You don't love your friends and family because of the way they look, do you? You love them because of who they are on the inside – and the same goes for you. People will like you for your personality, not your body.

THREE THINGS I LOVE ABOUT MYSELF...

DON'T compare yourself to others. This is the easiest way to end up feeling bad about yourself. We're all unique and we should embrace that.

Focus on the **GOOD**. If you're ever feeling bad about yourself, write down three **GOOD** things you like about you. It could be your gaming skills, your smile, or how great you are at maths – anything! The important thing is to focus on the positive.

BODY SHAMING

Body shaming is when someone makes <u>critical or negative</u> comments about the way someone looks, to their face or behind their back – and it's **NEVER OK**. In fact, body shaming is a form of <u>bullying</u> and sometimes people might not even realise they are doing it. This isn't just something girls have to deal with – guys are often made to believe they have to look a certain way too. Take a look at the following examples.

WHICH DO YOU THINK SHOW BODY SHAMING?
ANSWER: ALL OF THEM.

> YOU'LL NEVER PLAY FOOTBALL WITH THOSE CHICKEN LEGS, DANIEL

> JAMES IS TOO SHORT AND SKINNY TO JOIN OUR TEAM

> YOU SHOULD LOSE SOME WEIGHT, ABDUL – YOU'RE TOO CHUBBY

All the people mentioned above are being criticized about the way they look in some way. No, nope and **NOT OKAY**. Our differences are what make us human and our <u>differences are great</u>!

Aled's story, age 17

'I'M A BOY AND I WAS BODY SHAMED.'

'For about two years I was picked on every day for being 'too skinny'. The worst thing was that it was my friends making the comments. They didn't even realise they were being mean or making me feel bad – they'd just say things about my body in a jokey way, and all laugh about it. They made me feel like I was less of a boy because I wasn't as tall or as big as them. It took me a long time to realise that this was a form of bullying – and that there's no 'normal' way for a boy to look. I'm still slim, but now I'm not ashamed of that – it's who I am and that's OK.'

Beware of the media

Now that you know what body shaming is, you'll probably spot it in the media – that's newspapers, magazines, TV and films. Look out for anything that suggests there is a 'normal' or 'perfect' way for people to look. When you see it, shout **BODY SHAMING** inside your head (or out loud, if you feel like it), and remember that it's a load of nonsense.

SOCIAL MEDIA & PHONES

Social media is the name for websites and apps that let you share pictures, videos and messages with your friends and family. **INSTAGRAM**, **SNAPCHAT**, **FACEBOOK**, **WHATSAPP** and **TWITTER** are all different types of social media. Easy, right?

Staying safe online

DO keep your privacy settings **ON**, to make sure that only friends and family can see your posts.

DO block anyone who makes you uncomfortable or upset. A lot of apps have a 'report' button, so you can let them know if someone is being inappropriate or worrying.

DO remember that what you post on the internet is out there **FOREVER!** People can screenshot your pictures or comments, even if you delete them later.

TELL ME ALL ABOUT YOURSELF

Online life is <u>NOT</u> real life!

Social media can have a real effect on our lives. It might be that people from school are posting photos from a party, and you feel left out. Or perhaps those celebs (or even people you know) who seem to have perfect lives are making your life seem a bit rubbish in comparison.

It happens to **ALL** of us, but here's what you need to remember: online life is **NOT REAL LIFE**. People only post what they want you to see on social media – pretty pictures don't show how someone is feeling inside.

Beware...

DON'T have your full name as your username on sites like Instagram, Twitter, Snapchat etc.

DON'T add anyone you don't know. They might be pretending to be someone they're not to get close to you. Besides, do you really want a stranger seeing your pictures? **NOPE**.

DON'T give **ANYONE** your personal details. This includes your address, where you go to school, your surname and your passwords.

DON'T send anything to anyone you don't 100 per cent trust.

CYBERBULLYING

SOCIAL MEDIA is a great way for sharing and keeping in contact with your pals. But it has a dark side too, in the form of online bullying.

The problem with cyberbullying is that people can get to you constantly, at any time of the day, online. Whether you're chilling at home, or checking your phone on the bus, wherever you log in you are only fingertips away from abusive content. Not being able to escape from that is horrible, harmful and **NOT OK**.

Stupid!

So ugly.

Get a life.

Loser!

WHY ARE THEY BEING SO NASTY?

Am I being cyberbullied?

You might not even realise that you are being cyberbullied, because you think what's happening to you is normal. It's not. Here's what to look out for:

1. Mean photos or comments about you.

2. Nasty or upsetting comments on your posts.

3. Being ganged up on.

4. Dreading going online.

What to do

If you are being bullied in any way – online or otherwise – remember these four words: **DON'T SUFFER IN SILENCE**. You should never, ever, ever think that nobody will listen to you, or believe you, or help you – there is **ALWAYS** someone you can talk to. Look at the handy list below.

> PLEASE TELL ME WHAT'S WRONG

Who can I talk to?

1. A parent or adult that you trust.
2. An older brother or sister.
3. A teacher.
4. A school counsellor or peer advisor.
5. A close friend.

> THEY ARE SAYING HORRIBLE THINGS ABOUT ME ONLINE

Explain what's been going on and tell them how bad it's been making you feel. Save screengrabs of horrible comments or photos so that they can see for themselves. You could even keep a diary of events.

BULLYING & PEER PRESSURE

Bullying comes in different forms and is when someone targets another person with repeated, deliberate and unpleasant behaviour. Some people who bully might use physical strength to **INTIMIDATE** others, but it can also involve name-calling, or being excluded from a friendship group. Whatever form the bullying takes, if you are feeling 'got at', then you are being subjected to a form of bullying, and it is **NOT OK**.

Your school will have ways of dealing with this, so if you are being bullied – or think someone else is – **SPEAK UP**, and tell a teacher what's going on. There are also anti-bullying websites online that offer a safe space for advice and support.

What is a healthy friendship?

A FRIENDSHIP SHOULDN'T:

1. Make you feel bad about yourself.

2. Make you feel like you have to do or say things you don't want to.

3. Be hard work, or make you worry if you are liked.

A FRIENDSHIP SHOULD:

1. Be fun!

2. Be comfortable.

3. Be based on trust.

HA! HA! HA!

BACK IN CONTROL!

What is peer pressure?

'PEERS' are people who are your age, like your classmates. If they try and persuade you to do something, or you feel like you have to act a certain way to fit in, that's called 'peer pressure' – and it's **NOT OK**.

Peer pressure is...

1. Being encouraged to skip school. Bunking off won't just get you in trouble, but will also affect your learning, and your future – it's not worth it!

2. Being pressured to smoke cigarettes, drink alcohol or take drugs. All have a serious impact on your health. Whether or not you drink alcohol is a decision to make once you reach 18, but smoking and taking drugs – illegal or 'legal highs' – is ALWAYS really dangerous, and can lead to death. Just say no.

3. Being forced to join in with bullying, or leaving someone out. You might think that if you don't join in, you'll be left out next. This is a form of peer pressure.

4. Acting a certain way to fit in. Changing your normal behaviour so that you can join in and be 'cool' or popular is also peer pressure. Be yourself!

Always remember that it's **YOUR LIFE**, and these are **YOUR DECISIONS** to make. If someone told you to put your hand in a fire, you wouldn't. So why would you let someone decide what happens to you in another way? **EXACTLY**.

SCHOOL LIFE

School can be **HARD**, right? There are so many different lessons and you want to do well in all of them. You should always try your very best, but don't beat yourself up if you don't get top marks in everything.

> I WISH I KNEW THE ANSWER...

> I KNOW THIS ONE. IT'S EASY!

Everyone is good at different things. Paul might be a whizz at maths, but struggle in history. John might be the best at art, but not so great at science. People have different strengths, and that is a-ok.

If you're struggling, **NEVER** be afraid to ask your teacher for help. If they know you're finding something difficult, they can help you. That is their job, after all!

Too much pressure!

We've spoken about peer pressure, but parents can also put pressure on you, and that's difficult. Obviously you should <u>always</u> do your homework (even if it's a drag) but your life should have balance – there should be time for fun and relaxing after school too.

MY BEST IS NEVER GOOD ENOUGH

Feel like your **PARENTS** are expecting too much? Explain that you know they want you to be the best you can be, but make sure they realise that you're trying your hardest, and that you can't do more than that. Nobody (not even your parents!) should make you feel like you're not good enough. OK?

Dyslexia

Dyslexia is a learning condition that affects how the brain sees letters and symbols, making things like reading and telling the time super difficult. Support for dyslexia is very good these days, and your school will give you extra help if you're dyslexic. It's nothing to be embarrassed about and it doesn't mean you are any less intelligent than anyone else. In fact, dyslexics often have very **HIGH** intelligence. So there!

SEXISM & GENDER EQUALITY

What's better, being a boy or being a girl? Sorry, that was a trick question – because the answer is **BOTH**. Men and women may have different types of bodies, but does that mean one is better then the other? **NO** – of course not! Sexism is when people are treated unequally or are expected to act a certain way, just because of their gender (whether they're a girl or a boy).

Give me an example!

'Girls shouldn't play football – it's a boys' game!' This is an example of sexism. There is literally no reason why girls shouldn't play football, or any rule that says boys or girls have to like different things.

I'M A FOOTIE CHAMPION!

'Matt's crying like a girl' More sexism! It's totally normal for boys to cry if they're sad, and it doesn't make them any less male – that's an old-fashioned way of thinking.

'The woman should stay home with the kids while the man goes to work.' Sound the sexism alarm! Men and women are equally capable, equally intelligent and equally able to work. There are lots of stay-at-home dads and working mums too. It's down to individual choice.

What is a feminist?

Feminism is not about hating men – it is about believing that men and women are equal and should therefore be treated exactly the same in all areas of life. Everyone – men and women – should be a feminist, because equality of rights and opportunities is really important.

EQUAL RIGHTS

FEMINIST AND PROUD

EQUALITY FOR ALL

Did you know?

Less than 100 years ago women were not allowed to vote (and they still can't in some countries!), so we've come a long way since then. But there's still further to go. In a lot of workplaces, women still don't get paid the same as men, even when they do the same job! Ridiculous, right?

FAMILY TALK

There are loads of different family types: single-parent, foster, step-families, two mums or two dads or even being brought up by your grandparents, and no one family type is better than another. What's important is that a family is **LOVING** and **SUPPORTIVE** – even if you do argue sometimes, or slam your door when you're in a mood.

Marriage and divorce

When two people **LOVE** each other, they may decide to get married. But sometimes married people fall out of love and end the marriage, which is called 'getting a divorce'.

If your parents choose to get divorced, it can be very painful. It may seem like life as you know it is ending, and that can make you feel angry too.

REMEMBER

If your parents are getting divorced, don't keep all those feelings inside – it'll only make you feel worse. Talk to your parents, they'll help you understand why this is happening.

The important thing to keep in mind is that it's **NOT. YOUR. FAULT.** Divorce is a personal thing between two people; there's nothing you could have done to prevent it. Sometimes adults just fall out of love with each other – it's very sad, but it happens. Your parents will always love **YOU**, no matter what. Divorce doesn't change that.

Adoption

'Adoption' is when adults become the legal parents of a child they didn't give birth to. Being adopted isn't anything to be ashamed of – it makes you extra special because your parents CHOSE you. It also doesn't mean they are not really your parents: being a parent means supporting and loving a child as it grows. It doesn't matter if they made you or not.

Step-families

One or both of your parents might choose to get married again and their new wife or husband will be your step-mum or step-dad. If they already have children, these become step-brothers or step-sisters.

When two families come together, it is sometimes called a 'blended' family. It can be really great, but also difficult and strange. **ALWAYS** find someone to talk to about it all – don't try and muddle through on your own.

DEPRESSION

There's a **LOT** to deal with when you're growing up, and this can make you feel down or upset from time to time. However, sometimes all the changes you're going through, or problems at home and school, can lead to a more serious condition called <u>depression</u>.

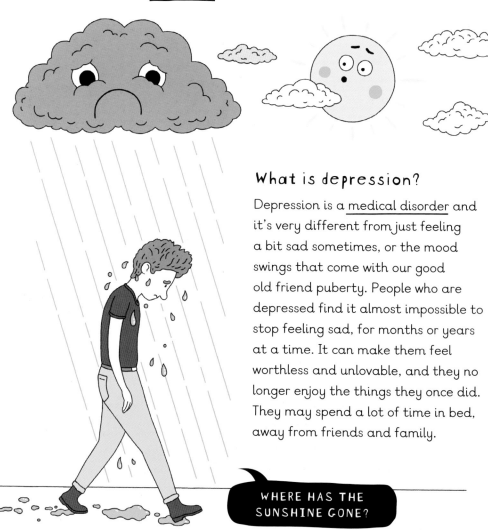

What is depression?

Depression is a <u>medical disorder</u> and it's very different from just feeling a bit sad sometimes, or the mood swings that come with our good old friend puberty. People who are depressed find it almost impossible to stop feeling sad, for months or years at a time. It can make them feel worthless and unlovable, and they no longer enjoy the things they once did. They may spend a lot of time in bed, away from friends and family.

WHERE HAS THE SUNSHINE GONE?

How do I deal with it?

Unlike a sore throat or a broken arm, depression is a **MENTAL ILLNESS**, and there's no quick cure — you can't put a cast on someone's brain!

Doctors **CAN** treat depression, though, with medication and therapy. If you think you might be depressed, or feel like you want to hurt yourself, please, **PLEASE** speak to someone. Left untreated it will only get worse, so you **MUST** ask for help. We promise you — it **WILL** get better.

Josh's story, age 12

'IT TOOK ME A LONG TIME TO REALISE I WAS DEPRESSED'

'I just never felt happy anymore. Even things I used to enjoy — like playing Playstation with all the guys — didn't get rid of my feeling of utter sadness. All I wanted to do was lie in bed in the dark and sleep, because at least when I was asleep I wasn't feeling so terrible. I didn't want to see or talk to anyone — I even thought about hurting myself. Thankfully my mum realised what was going on and took me to a doctor who diagnosed me with depression. Now I'm getting treatment, including seeing a therapist once a week to talk things through, and it's really helping.'

I'M HERE TO HELP

GROWING UP HAPPY

Growing up isn't always easy. In fact, it can be the hardest time of your life. Your body and emotions change so quickly – in ways that are probably quite bewildering – that sometimes you struggle to keep up!

WE DID IT TOGETHER!

We hope that this book has given you some idea of what to expect from puberty and how to cope with everything that comes with it – and if there's one thing you should remember, it's this: **YOU CAN DO IT!**

For support & advice*

CHILDLINE: 0800 1111
www.childline.org.uk

NATIONAL BULLYING HELPLINE:
07734 701 221
www.nationalbullyinghelpline.co.uk

THE SAMARITANS: 116 123
www.samaritans.org

SWITCHBOARD LGBT+ HELPLINE:
0300 330 0630
www.switchboard.lgbt

Who can help?

The best piece of advice we can give you is never go it alone. If you're struggling, **TALK TO SOMEONE.** That can be a trusted adult, a friend or a trained professional. Here are some websites and helplines that can help:

* CHILDREN SHOULD BE SUPERVISED WHEN USING THE INTERNET, PARTICULARLY WHEN USING AN UNFAMILIAR WEBSITE FOR THE FIRST TIME. THE PUBLISHERS AND AUTHOR CANNOT BE RESPONSIBLE FOR THE CONTENT OF THE WEBSITES REFERRED TO IN THIS BOOK.

Positive puberty

REMEMBER that you're not the first person to have felt this way, or to have gone through puberty. Every single adult you see dealt with the P-word and came out the other side — you can too!

SAY 'I am strong and powerful and I can deal with anything' three times, out loud. Yes, you might feel a bit silly, but it actually works.

DO SOMETHING that makes you howl with laughter — whether it's watching your fave TV show, being silly with a friend or tickling your little brother until he's wheezing.

WRITE DOWN three things you like about yourself, however small. If you're feeling sad or down, look at this list and remember why you are special.

REMEMBER that EVERYONE is different, and that's what makes the world go round. Difference is good, difference makes us human.

CONFIDENCE IS KEY. We don't mean being loud, or the centre of attention — but having confidence in yourself, and who you are. Love yourself, and the world will too.

You are a strong, **BRILLIANT** and amazing human being, taking your first steps down the road to adulthood and the rest of your life. That's exciting, and even if there are a few bumps and hurdles along the way, just keep walking down that road — you **WILL** get through it all.

GLOSSARY

ACNE Medically known as *Acne Vulgaris*, acne is a skin disease caused by infected or inflamed oil glands at the base of hair follicles.

ANOREXIA NERVOSA A serious illness / eating disorder characterized by an obsessive desire to lose weight and extreme dieting.

ANUS The hole in your bottom that solid waste (poo) passes through when you go to the toilet.

BODY IMAGE How you see yourself – the subjective or mental image of your own body.

BODY SHAMING Making critical or negative comments about someone based on their size or weight, or what they look like.

BULIMIA NERVOSA A serious illness / eating disorder characterized by intentionally vomiting food shortly after eating.

BULLYING The repetitive, intentional hurting of one person or group by another person or group, where the relationship involves an imbalance of power.

CERVIX The entrance to the uterus at the top of a woman's vagina.

CIRCUMCISION The removal of a fold of skin, known as the foreskin, that surrounds the head (glans) of the un-erect penis.

CLITORIS A sensitive bump, just above the opening to the vagina, that feels nice when it's touched gently.

CONTRACEPTION Methods for preventing pregnancy.

EJACULATION The release of semen from the penis at orgasm (sexual climax), during sex.

ERECTION The hardening of the penis that occurs when sponge-like tissue inside the penis fills up with blood.

FALLOPIAN TUBES The tubes leading from the ovaries to the uterus.

FOLLICLES Tiny holes in your skin from which hairs grow.

FORESKIN The fold of smooth skin and tissue that surrounds and protects the head (glans) of the penis.

GLAND A cell or organ that makes chemical substances and then releases them into the body.

HORMONE A chemical substance made by glands and then transported around the body.

OESTROGEN A hormone, mainly produced by the ovaries, that develops the female body.

OVARIES The female reproductive organs, which produce eggs.

PENIS The male genital organ that releases semen and urine from the body.

PITUITARY GLAND A pea-sized gland at the base of the brain that releases hormones.

PUBERTY The process which takes place when a child's body gradually changes into an adult's body.

PUBIC BONE A protective bone at the front of the pelvis.

PUBIC HAIR Hair covering your pubic bone.
SMEGMA A whitish substance of dead skin cells and skin oils that can build up under the foreskin.

TESTICLES Male sex glands that store sperm behind the penis in a pouch of skin called the scrotum.

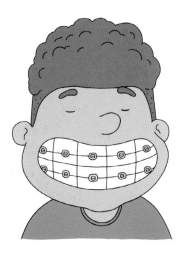

TESTOSTERONE A hormone produced by the testes that tells the male body how to develop and change.

URETHRA A tiny tube that takes urine (wee) from the bladder to the outside of your body. The end of the urethra forms a small opening in your body just above the vagina (if you are a girl) or at the end of the penis (if you are a boy).

UTERUS A hollow organ within the abdomen of a woman, in which a baby grows. Also known as a 'womb'.

VAGINA The tube that leads from a woman's cervix to an outer opening, in between the urethra and anus. It is very stretchy so a baby can come out.

VERRUCAS Small painful warts on the soles of your feet.

VULVA The lips at the opening of the vagina.

WET DREAMS Ejaculating while asleep.

INDEX

A GUIDE FOR GROWN-UPS

Puberty doesn't just affect those going through it — it can also be a **CHALLENGING** and daunting time for families and teachers. This book is designed to help not only boys making the transformation from child to adult, but also you.

It can be a great idea to read this book together. For you, it can act as a guide on how to discuss the physical and emotional changes that come with puberty. For a child, it allows time to ask **QUESTIONS** about puberty and all that comes with it.

If your son or pupil wants to read this book alone, suggest having a chat afterwards to answer any questions he might have.

Sometimes boys can find it difficult to seek advice, and so end up trying to deal with things alone. Let him know that he can **TALK** to you whenever he needs to. Just being aware that he has your support is invaluable, even if he doesn't always feel like sharing or opening up.

Both men and women have an important role in influencing a young boy's health, well-being and the way in which he comes to view the opposite sex. So be **CONFIDENT** in your approach to the content in this book, teaching him that talking openly and never being embarrassed to ask for advice or help is the foundation to growing up happy.

TEACHERS are incredibly important, too. Check that your school policy, which should be developed in consultation with parents and pupils, supports you when teaching and answering questions. If you feel it needs updating or amending, set the wheels in motion and make this happen!

LET'S LOOK AT THIS TOGETHER

Lead the way

How we act and behave can affect a young boy's perception of the world, and how he interacts with others. By being sensitive, caring and open, we can try to break down some of the stereotypes surrounding manhood.